HAZING
in High Schools
Causes and Consequences

**Kevin L. Guynn
and
Frank D. Aquila**

CONTRA COSTA COUNTY LIBRARY
Phi Delta Kappa Educational Foundation
Bloomington, Indiana U.S.A.

Cover design by
Victoria Voelker

Phi Delta Kappa Educational Foundation
408 North Union Street
Post Office Box 789
Bloomington, IN 47402-0789
U.S.A.

Printed in the United States of America
Library of Congress Control Number 2004115433
ISBN 0-87367-855-9

TABLE OF CONTENTS

WHAT IS HAZING?

May 2003 will be remembered in the Glenbrook North High School community in suburban Chicago, and likely elsewhere, for a highly disturbing sort of tragedy. What happened at Glenbrook North did not result in any student deaths, but it did shine a national spotlight on a problem that arises in schools, particularly high schools, across the nation: hazing.

The Glenbrook hazing incident occurred at a "powder puff" football game and was captured on videotape, which was aired on a local television station before making national television news. It showed 12th-grade girls pushing, punching, and smearing paint and excrement on their 11th-grade classmates. One junior girl needed stitches to close a head wound, and another suffered a broken ankle. A wave of disbelief and outrage rippled across the country, and many school people found themselves asking, "Could it happen here?"

Although the event took place off school grounds and not during school hours, school officials were determined to have jurisdiction and disciplined students by suspending them from classes. The police also were involved, and one mother subsequently was charged with supplying alcohol. Lawsuits were brought, and the negative press continued for weeks. What was supposed to have been an informal football game in which the senior girls play the junior girls was an instance of hazing.

The hazing incident in Glenbrook, Illinois, is unusual only in its intensity. Hazing is the exercise of control or power, usually in a punitive or abusive manner, by persons who are members of a group or organization and directed at individuals seeking admission to the group. Hazing often is an initiation ritual. The Fraternity Insurance Purchasing Group defines hazing as:

> any action taken or situation created, intentionally . . . to produce or cause mental or physical discomfort, embarrassment, harassment, or ridicule. Such activities may include

but are not limited to the following: use of alcohol; paddling in any form; creation of excessive fatigue; physical and psychological shocks; quests, treasure hunts, scavenger hunts, road trips; . . . kidnappings; . . . wearing of public apparel which is conspicuous and not normally in good taste; engaging in public stunts and buffoonery; morally degrading or humiliating games and activities; and any other activities which are not consistent with academic achievement, fraternal law, ritual or policy, or the regulations and policies of the educational institution, or applicable state law. [1]

Hazing has a long history. In the past, hazing was more acceptable than it is today. But, like many rituals, hazing initiations conflict with the current societal norms of acceptance and openness. Hazing is at odds with the public rhetoric that largely espouses tolerance and nonviolence. And yet it persists.

In fact, once considered a practice confined to college fraternities and sororities, hazing has become all too familiar in high schools across the United States. A national survey published in August 2000 by Alfred University[2] found that of the 91% of high school students who participated in group activities, 48% admitted having participated in hazing activities. Twenty-nine percent admitted doing things that were potentially illegal as part of their initiation into a group. The study concluded that every high school student who joins a group, including theater groups, church groups, football teams, and the band, is at risk of being hazed.

The definition of hazing offered by the Fraternity Insurance Purchasing Group is one among many. It is useful but not universal. High school authorities often are faced with the task of determining whether a particular activity or action is hazing or something else, perhaps a practical joke. In general, two conditions must be present for an activity to be defined as hazing. First, the actions of those accused of hazing must be directed at an individual (or group of individuals) who is attempting to gain admittance to a group or organization. Second, a dominant individual or group must exert control over a subservient individual or group. In most cases, individuals in the group to which admittance is sought determine what those persons who seek admittance must do in order to be permitted to join.

Features of Hazing

Hazing can involve physical or psychological abuse, or both. Some hazed students have endured humiliation; they have been shouted at, called names, or demeaned in other ways. Others have been physically assaulted; they have been paddled, stripped, smeared with urine or feces, or made to drink vile-tasting concoctions. Sexual assaults are not uncommon as forms of hazing. And sadly, a number of adolescents have died as a result of hazing.

Although the detrimental effects are not as visible, psychological hazing has the potential for being as dangerous as physical hazing. For example, psychological hazing occurs when an initiate is placed in a situation that he or she believes to be more dangerous or embarrassing than it really is. Individuals have been blindfolded and made to jump from what they believed to be a high point, which, in fact, was only inches above the ground. The danger in such an instance is not the fall, but the stress of uncertainty.

Sexual hazing also can be psychological. For example, an individual may be blindfolded and made to kneel. There is the sound of a zipper, and the initiate is instructed to kiss what he (usually a male) supposes to be the genitals of the hazer. In fact, the "genitals" are a hotdog. Too often, however, hazing is, or proceeds to, real sexual assault, rather than pretended sexual assault.

What may not cause mental anguish in one person may be extremely troubling to another. For example, a group of upperclassmen hazed a black female student attending band camp by dressing in robes similar to those associated with the Ku Klux Klan.[3] The added racial overtones of this hazing incident might not have had the same effect if the initiate had been white. The ritual produced heightened anxiety because the victim was black — and it led to a lawsuit.

It bears mention that hazing tends to be contextualized. Initiation into a show choir, for example, might involve singing; hazing by a track team might involve making the initiates run for a long distance. Context also extends to the location of the hazing. The track team hazing activity likely would be set on a track or playing field.

Because hazing has existed as ritual over time, many forms of hazing follow tradition. Organizations "pass down" their hazing rituals. In fact, tradition is a key reason why hazing persists. Those who are hazed as initiates one year become the hazers the next year. Unfortunately, as a tradition persists, over time the bar often is raised; the ritual is intensified. What was scary or shocking becomes passé, and so new twists must be added. It should not be surprising that some hazing rituals move from the innocuous to the dangerous and even the deadly.

There is another factor to consider: Hazing rituals usually are secret, though the degree of secrecy varies. In many cases hazing rituals come to light only after someone is injured. Once that happens, school authorities, parents, and others become involved. Often they are taken by surprise to discover that hazing has been occurring. If a hazing incident results in injury or death, or if the hazing circumstances are sufficiently offensive to societal norms, then there will be legal ramifications and, likely, community outrage.[4]

The purpose of this short guidebook is to consider hazing in high schools. What are the causes of hazing, and what are the consequences? If educators understand hazing, then they can work to eliminate it. Before hazing becomes an issue, school boards need to review policies and practices. Appropriate policies can minimize the incidence of hazing.[5] But policies alone will be ineffective without proactive vigilance by parents and educators who are willing to communicate and collaborate with one another. Unaddressed hazing compromises the ethical character of the learning community, exposes students to physical and psychological dangers, and makes the schools liable in cases of harm.

CHAPTER ONE

A Brief History of Hazing

Hazing can be traced to the Middle Ages. As towns and cities began to expand beyond the castle walls, the guild movement flourished across Europe. Craftsmen, in effect, unionized to protect jobs and control the marketplace by controlling who was able to practice a trade, such as goldsmithing. The guilds were not just keepers of knowledge, but also schools. Masters passed along their skills to apprentices, who in turn became masters in their own right and took on their own apprentices. Guilds became powerful organizations, and rituals of initiation were held when newcomers were admitted.

Guilds and religious orders became models for other types of organizations, such as secret societies and fraternities. According to William Joseph Whalen, college fraternal organizations began to flourish in the United States in the 1800s.[6] Fraternities, secret societies, military groups, and voluntary organizations often used rituals (including passwords, symbols, handshakes) to instill moral or religious values. These organizations and their rituals became the models for college fraternities, which, in turn, became models for similar groups at the high school level.

The first fraternities in high schools were literary organizations, which served an educational purpose. Over time, however, fraternities at both secondary and postsecondary levels came to emphasize the social over the academic. And in the late 1800s and early 1900s, high school fraternities were joined by secret societies. According to surveys conducted in 1904, between 40% and 50% of American high schools could boast at least one fraternity or sorority, with participation ranging from 8% to 36% of the student body.[7]

Taking into account most of the various student organizations, these largely social groups were, and still are, modeled on their college and adult counterparts. There often have been direct links between the adult and adolescent levels. Some of these organizations continue today. For example, Kiwanis Clubs are adult organizations dedicated to community service and good citizenship, values also imparted through their high school Key Clubs, which strive to build character and foster leadership in teenagers. In addition, members of such organizations as the Masons and DeMolay International have created systems so that adults provide role models for youngsters to follow in order to develop and practice what the organization deems as positive attributes. The models these organizations follow are designed to introduce the youths to a particular way of life and have them see the adult member living that lifestyle.

Most high school fraternities, sororities, and clubs — then and now — follow certain guidelines. They elect officers and pursue projects as prescribed by their own and the school's rules and regulations. Many of these groups provide valuable experiences for young people, and their work can be helpful to the school and the community.

Secret societies, on the other hand, have tended to be a different matter. In some cases, fraternities and sororities have been included in this category of organization, depending on the nature of their membership and activities. During World War II, many fraternal organizations (including secret societies) reached their membership peak; and then there was a backlash, particularly against the secret societies. Such organizations came to be seen as separatist and exclusionary, and thus detrimental to the secondary school ethos. Students who took part in such organizations were viewed as cliquish, and the societies were seen as breeding grounds for delinquent behavior. School boards and administrators tried to discourage secret societies by imposing penalties for participation and outright bans. The number of schools banning such organizations grew steadily during the 1940s and 1950s. (See Appendix B: Chronology of Cases Related to Secret Societies.)

Students and parents sometimes objected to a school's ban on secret societies, but the courts repeatedly upheld the right of school boards to restrict such groups, whether by the imposition of strict guidelines on the groups or by policies that forbid their formation. By the 1960s most American high schools had eliminated fraternities, sororities, and secret societies from their campuses. However, formally banning such groups did not eliminate the practices associated with them, such as exclusionary membership, secrecy, and rituals, including hazing.

Students invariably stratify themselves according to interests, class, race, physical ability, and other characteristics. The decade of the 1960s also was a period of youth rebellion and social upheaval in the United States. And so, by the 1970s college fraternities and sororities, which had retained their status, were enjoying new freedoms associated with the greater openness in society. Some postsecondary fraternal organizations also intensified their initiation rituals in response to this openness. In many cases, high school groups mimicked them, and hazing soon became interwoven with participation in any form of youth organization.

No longer viewed simply as youthful hijinks, hazing is now seen as a serious matter. Indeed, hazing often is more violent now than in the past. The danger to young people has increased, and so the response from schools, the courts, and society in general also has become stronger.

Responsibility and Liability

In the 1940s, in *Ohman* v. *Board of Education of the City of New York* the court concluded, "Parents do not send their children to school to be returned to them maimed because of the absence of proper supervision or the abandonment of supervision."[8] This standard has not changed. Clearly, it is the responsibility of the school to ensure that students are not harmed by hazing. When students are harmed because school officials have failed to act in a proper manner, then the school is liable.

Unfortunately, it too often takes a dramatic hazing incident to motivate school officials to examine their policies and practices. Such was the case in California in 2000 when students at Righetti High School attacked another student on a school bus in what was characterized as a hazing incident gone awry.[9] A 15-year-old freshman boy was kicked, punched, and partially undressed by several upperclassmen as the students were returning from a track meet. One attacker grabbed the boy's crotch and simulated a sex act. The victim passed out from the beating. The bus driver and the coach riding the bus claimed not to have seen or heard the incident.

The attack came to light when the victim's parents got involved. Four students were suspended for taking part in the incident; two were later expelled. After the incident, school officials belatedly reviewed their policies on hazing and instituted better supervision measures. The school got off easier than the attackers in terms of legal consequences in this case, though questions lingered in the media and in some parents' minds about how school officials might have prevented the hazing.

Other schools have faced greater consequences after hazing incidents. In Chapter Two we discuss some of the legal actions that have resulted from other incidents of hazing "gone awry."

Why Hazing Persists

Hazing has not disappeared. Many states have passed antihazing statutes, but reports of hazing incidents would suggest that state policy makers have not yet been effective in eliminating the problem. However, any attempt to evaluate the effectiveness of such statutes raises more questions. With an antihazing statute in place, does an increase in reported incidents indicate the ineffectiveness of the statute, shoddy enforcement, or simply a higher level of reporting than was previously the case? The same questions apply at the school level. When schools institute rules against hazing and more hazing incidents are reported, what are we to make of it?

Determining why hazing persists is not an easy task, but looking beyond the actual hazing events can help. It is useful to examine developmental issues and to analyze the cycle of hazing. High school hazing occurs at a time in the lives of hazers and victims alike when they are exploring their interactions with peers. Young persons who submit themselves to hazing do so because they seek to belong to a group, though the ritual may be borne reluctantly. Hazers can be persuasive or coercive in order to maintain a group's "tradition." For example, a senior may say to a freshman, in effect, "Everyone who joins the track team is initiated. If you want to be part of this team, you will go along with this. If you don't, you won't make the team." The reality is that the initiation ritual has nothing to do with "making the team"; it is a rite of passage that must be endured to *belong* to the group.

In some cases, hazers give their victims the option to "volunteer" to be hazed. Other times, the hazers, almost always slightly older students than their victims, initiate the ritual without forewarning. This can proceed from an implicit "understanding" that enduring the ritual hazing is a norm for joining the group. When school administrators are unaware of hazing rituals or look the other way, this norm becomes institutionalized.

The idea of normalizing or institutionalizing ritual hazing points up the notion that hazing is a belief system or, perhaps more accurately, embodies a set of beliefs that may or may not be systematic in practice. Four perspectives are useful to examine these beliefs: tradition, attitudes, process, and context.

Tradition offers guidelines. Our traditions are our comfort zones. For example, holiday traditions guide us in how to behave and what to expect during a particular season. They provide an aspect of social-emotional leveling. Tradition takes precedence over individual desires. Tradition urges the belief that it is better, or easier, to "go along to get along." Thus tradition provides a formula for making the best of what might be a trying or challenging event, whether it is eating a holiday dinner with the family or attending a funeral. Tradition bonds through the sharing of experiences. And thus traditions endure. They get passed from old to young.

Tradition, whether positive or negative, plays a major role in many hazing activities. Stories take on mythic attributes — what happened during a particular football game or at band camp — and form a basis for hazing activities that replicate or reenact the stories. Other traditions involve real or symbolic shows of bravery. For example, a group may demand that an initiate eat a raw egg or swallow a live goldfish. Hazing activities that begin innocently become intensified as veterans of hazing add new dimensions. Eating one egg becomes eating five.

Attitudes associate hazing with rights and responsibilities. Those who have been hazed believe that they have the right — even the duty — to haze others. Many who haze believe that hazing is a good thing, an attitude with historical precedents. Martin Luther espoused the belief that older students should initiate a young man in order for the youth to prove his worth and mettle. As a West Point cadet, Douglas MacArthur was made to do deep knee bends over broken glass as part of his initiation hazing. MacArthur, who later gained fame as a World War II general, eventually fell unconscious and suffered from convulsions.[10] His superiors demanded that MacArthur tell them which upperclassmen were involved and what had transpired. MacArthur refused because he was bonding with the other students and his sense of loyalty to them was strong. Attitudes such as these make hazing, even when it becomes dangerous, difficult to eradicate. Institutionalized attitudes of acceptance with regard to hazing kept MacArthur from being charged with insubordination.

Attitudes of acceptance still play a role in how hazing incidents are treated. An incident that occurred in a Wisconsin high school offers an example. Several parents filed suit in the U.S. District Court after the school district disciplined five senior football players who admitted to paddling several sophomores at a party attended by some 200 students. Although other students were involved, the parents of the hazers alleged that only the football players were disciplined. The athletic director recommended community service for the football players, but the superintendent decided to suspend the players for two football games. The superintendent did not suspend the students from academic classes. The parents of the hazers chose to file suit in federal court, rather than appeal to the board of education. The parents' attorney said, "They didn't want to see a local government playing roughshod over kids accused of wrongdoing."[11] Some hazed students also wanted their abusers to do community service, rather than be suspended from games. In the end, the insurance company for the school district settled out of court, paying the parents $7,000, rather than risking a larger damage settlement in the jury trial.

Process takes hazing toward the psychological dimension. One goes through the process of hazing in order to prove willingness to abide by a certain code of conduct and to build trust and loyalty with the members of a group. The hazers are on one side and the initiates are on the other in this process. The psychological need to belong to the group provides the incentive for initiates to accept humiliation and degradation as means to prove their desire and "fitness" to join the group. The hazers, who already belong to the group, also have a stake in maintaining the values, principles, and exclusivity of the group. By hazing initiates, the members winnow prospective members, sorting out those individuals whom they perceive to share their values.

Raymond Schroth, a journalist writing on fraternities and the Greek system, began researching hazing in the mid-1980s. He believes that attempts to halt hazing will continue to fail because fraternities (and similar groups) have little purpose other than bonding and can survive only by reinforcing their traditions.[12] He further theorizes that pain is a key. The pain one class inflicts on another results in the formation of a physical-psychological bond. "Help weeks" (marked by community service) instead of "hell weeks" (marked by hazing), for example, do not engender the same level of bonding.

Lionel Tiger, an authority on male bonding, suggests that hazing often occurs in male-dominated social systems. Males subject themselves to hazing as a symbolic way of breaking ties to family and bonding to other males (the group) who possess like values. The hierarchy of the group replaces the hierarchy of family.[13]

Context is the dimension of hazing that incorporates the other three dimensions: tradition, attitudes, and process. Hazing falls within the context of basic needs, more strongly during certain ages than others. Throughout life, an individual will move from one group to another. These groups may be family, community, club, school, class, fraternity, and many others. The need to belong to some group, or several groups, is strong in most people throughout life. Indeed, in Maslow's Hierarchy of Needs, security and social needs come just after bodily needs, such as food, water, and sleep.[14] Particularly during adolescence and young adulthood, the need to belong to a group — to fit in with peers, for example — can be so powerful as to override reasonable caution and thus lead to dangerous hazing activities. The context of hazing is a basic needs context. Tradition, attitudes, and process converge, therefore, often leaving propriety and common sense behind.

The need to be an accepted member of a group that is believed to be prestigious and powerful can be an overwhelming force for young people. Adolescents in particular create their self-image and acquire self-worth not only through individual, personal accomplishment, but also through group affiliation. Flowers and Bolmeier write:

> For all ages, the most forceful drive is the drive for prestige and power connected with a social organization, but at no time is it so strong as at adolescence, when physical changes make it very necessary for the individual to have emotional security and status in the eyes of others. It is at this time that the child loses interest in adult-sponsored activities such as Boy Scouts and church groups and seeks the smaller, more homogeneous intimate group. If the group has an aura of mystery and glamour, and it is known that only the "best group" belongs, he will do everything in his power to become one of that group.[15]

This need to belong is perhaps the key reason why hazing continues to occur in high schools across the nation. Many students' desire to belong is so strong that it overrides all sensible thought, to the point that they will do anything to achieve this goal. This includes participating in activities in which they would not normally participate.

The eradication of hazing is further hampered by under-reporting, not only of hazing events but also of injuries related to hazing. An individual's need to belong may, in that person's mind and in the view of those in the group to which the individual is seeking admittance, outweigh society's need to know about the abuses of hazing. Therefore, on pain of losing peer acceptance, a student may keep quiet — about a bruise, a cut, a sprain, even a broken bone.[16] In fact, according to the Mayo Clinic, a majority of individuals injured during hazing activities do not seek medical attention.[17] This code of silence is difficult to break.

The inevitable conclusion is that hazing persists because both hazers and those hazed feel that it must.

CHAPTER TWO

An Overview of Legal Issues

Most hazing cases fall under the legal umbrella of tort actions. A tort occurs when one person injures another person. *Black's Law Dictionary* defines a tort as "a civil wrong for which a remedy may be obtained in the form of damages."[18] Specific types of torts that may be relevant in hazing situations include: 1) a government tort that is committed by the government through an employee or agent, 2) an intentional tort that may be committed by someone acting with general and specific intent, 3) a negligent tort that is committed by failure to observe the standard of care required by the law under the circumstances, and 4) a personal tort that involves an injury to one's person, reputation, or feelings.[19]

In order to comprehend fully the potential liabilities associated with hazing cases, it is important to understand the basic concepts related to torts. School officials do not directly injure students in hazing cases. Rather, students may be injured through negligence on the part of school officials. Negligence is a type of a nonintentional tort. *Black's Law Dictionary* defines negligence as:

> the failure to exercise the standard of care that a reasonably prudent person would have exercised in a similar situation; and conduct that falls below the legal standard established to protect others against unreasonable risk of harm, except for conduct that is intentionally, wantonly, or willfully disregardful of others' rights.[20]

The four elements of a negligent tort are duty of care, breach of that duty, proximate causation, and actual injury. A court will examine both the sequence of events and the elements of a tort to determine if all of the necessary components are in place when deciding if a tort has been committed, potential remedies, or possible defenses. Generally, four basic questions are asked:

First, was there a duty owed to the victim? If the answer to the first question is yes, then the second question is: Did the person or organization owing that duty breach the duty? If the answer to the second question is yes, then the third question arises: What caused the injury and was the defendant the proximate causation? Finally, the last question deals with whether or not an actual injury occurred. We will consider each of these tort elements.

Duty means that a person owes a legal responsibility to another to act in a certain way. A duty is an enforceable obligation to conform to a particular standard of conduct. In personal injury cases, courts determine the establishment of any duty using a "reasonable person" standard. In other words, what would a person of ordinary prudence do in similar circumstances? *Featherston* v. *Allstate Insurance*, 875 P.2d 937 (Idaho 1994), delineates duty of care and performance of that duty. The court described duty and the associated responsibility as: "if one voluntarily undertakes to perform an act, having no prior duty to do so, the duty arises to perform the act in a non-negligent manner."[21] In a school setting, an example of duty would be a teacher who agrees to supervise the school play. That teacher has the duty to supervise the students participating in the play. Administrators, parents, and the community expect the teacher to perform that duty in a non-negligent manner. The standard would be based on how a reasonable teacher, under the circumstances, would handle the play supervision.

Breach of duty occurs when one who has a duty to others acts contrary to or fails to act in the manner required by their duty, for example, a teacher leaves a classroom unattended in order to talk with another teacher. A breach can result from either a direct or an indirect series of actions, or inactions, that result in the injury of a person. Such injury may be a physical injury, a financial loss, or a violation of legal rights. Using the example of the teacher supervising the students during a play, a breach of duty might involve the teacher allowing piles of nail-laden wood from old stage flats to be haphazardly placed behind the stage. If during a rehearsal the teacher calls for the stage to be darkened and a student falls on the lumber pile, a breach may have occurred. If a reasonable teacher, under these same circumstances, would have removed the wood before darkening the stage, then the failure to remove the wood would be a breach of duty to supervise the students in a non-negligent way.

Proximate causation means that an injured party must be able to prove that the injury resulted because of the negligent act of the other party. Following are three cases that illustrate proximate causation and injury in various ways:

In *Sovereign Camp, W.O.W.* v. *Banks*, 170 So. 634 (Miss. 1936), the question was whether the Woodmen of the World, a fraternal society and a sponsor of Sovereign Camp, was responsible for a hazing injury that occurred after the conclusion of a prescribed initiation ritual. The case was heard in the Supreme Court of Mississippi after the trial court found that the sponsors of the camp owed Bennie Lee Banks, a camper, a duty of care after extending the prescribed ritual by paddling him. Banks' injury occurred when an employee of the camp and another camper struck Banks with a paddle nicknamed "the spanker." One side of the device was a paddle and the other had a metal cylinder encasing a blank cartridge. The intended purpose of this device was to allow the user to strike the individual with the padded side. This, in turn, would explode the cartridge on the other side, frightening the hazed individual. During the paddling, Magee struck Banks with the wrong side of the paddle, which caused the cartridge to tear a hole in Bank's buttocks. One of the issues before the court was the timing of the event. Evidence indicated that the ritualistic ceremony and the subsequent initiation administered by Martin and Magee were so close in time and unbroken as to indicate that they occurred at the same time. Therefore the extension of the initiation was the proximate cause of the injury.

In *Soares* v. *Lakeville,* 343 N.E.2d 840 (Mass. 1976), the father of the victim filed suit to recover for personal injuries and expenses incurred for his son's medical care. The victim, a 14-year-old boy, sustained injuries during an accident after a hazing incident at a summer camp. As the boy left a camp cabin, he fell and put his arm through the glass panel of a door. The appeals court examined whether the evidence, viewed in the light most favorable to the student, would support his cause of action. The court found no causal connection between the hazing and the accident. However, the court stated that if the older students had goaded the boy into heedless flight, a causal connection might have been found.

In *Chappel* v. *Franklin Pierce School District 402,* 426 P.2d 471 (Wash. 1967), staff members assumed supervisory roles over extracurricular student organizations. Upperclassmen injured James Chappel during an initiation ceremony held off school grounds. School authorities knew that students would be holding the initiation ceremony but did nothing to stop it. Thus, by not acting or even objecting, the school officials gave tacit approval. The appeals court found that the potential for injury was foreseeable from this type of activity. In essence, the court held that the school officials had the responsibility to stop the initiation ceremony because a prudent school authority should understand that allowing it to occur would place those in attendance in harm's way.

Actual injury involves another tort test. An injured party must prove that he or she actually was injured in some way by another party. *DeGooyer* v. *Harkness,* 13 N.W.2d 815 (S.D. 1944) involved a faculty member taking an active role in an initiation. With the approval of the superintendent, an athletic coach participated in an initiation ceremony involving high school athletes.

The initiation ceremony involved running electricity through the bodies of the students. After being shocked, Gerald DeGooyer, a student athlete, died. DeGooyer's family sued both the athletic director and the superintendent. The court found the athletic coach negligent in the death of DeGooyer. However, the court found that the superintendent's involvement was primarily centered on permitting the coach to hold the ceremony on school property. The court, therefore, found that the superintendent was not negligent in the student's death. It should be noted that this is a case from the 1940s. The holding, especially with regard to the superintendent, might be seen in a far different light in today's court system.

In a somewhat more recent case, the District Court of Appeals of Florida heard *Leahy* v. *School Board of Hernando County*, 450 So.2d 883 (Fla. 1984), a tort liability case, in which an injury occurred during a football drill. *Leahy* involved freshmen football players who had not been issued the proper equipment but were, nonetheless, engaging in practice drills with their older teammates. As the drills continued, the veterans began hitting harder and acting extremely rowdy. For instance, if a freshman player was knocked to the ground during a drill, a veteran player would knock the freshman back down to the ground as he attempted to stand back up. The veteran players' actions against the freshmen players were found to be hazing. The coach might have been able to lessen the school's exposure to liability if he had anticipated the actions of the veteran players. In its decision, the court referred to *Rupp* v. *Bryant*, 417 So.2d 658 (Fla.1982), concerning anticipation of student actions. In *Rupp*, the court found that certain student misbehavior is foreseeable and therefore is not an intervening cause that would relieve principals or teachers from liability for failure to supervise. (See discussion later in this chapter.) *Rupp* also espoused a major consideration concerning staff responsibility:

> we should not close our eyes to the fact that . . . boys of
> seventeen and eighteen years of age, particularly in groups
> where the herd instinct and competitive spirit tend naturally

to relax vigilance, are not accustomed to exercise the same amount of care for their own safety as persons of more mature years.[22]

Recognizing that one main task of adult supervisors is to anticipate and curb student misbehavior, courts often have held that failure to prevent injuries caused by the intentional or reckless conduct of the victim or another student may constitute negligence. *Leahy* is important to school employees for several reasons. First, the duty of care element is evident. The coaching staff assumed the responsibility to provide the students with proper equipment. In this case, the breach of duty involved not only the failure to issue the freshmen players helmets (an inaction) but also allowing these students to participate in drills with veteran students wearing full equipment (an action). The court also considered the fact that the coaches were in the area during the time of the injury but did not halt the hazing.

Second, consideration must be given to the extent to which the students were engaged in the activity. The court determined this incident was hazing, partly because the situation involved veteran players aggressively attacking a group of younger students. The court could not find that the activity undertaken by the veteran players allowed these boys to bond into a stronger team. Rather, the court found that the adults in charge failed to anticipate the aggression and put a halt to it before an injury occurred.

Another example is *Caldwell* v. *Griffin Spalding County Board of Education*, 1998 GA. 111 (Ga. 1998). Antwan Caldwell claimed that the school board, the football coach, and the principal all knew or should have known that "initiations" were an annual event. Caldwell, a freshman on the Griffin High School varsity football team, was attacked and beaten by other members of the team during an apparent initiation ritual that took place at the team's summer football camp. In this case, the board of education successfully argued that sovereign immunity and official immunity protected them. The appellate courts of the state of Georgia had consistently held that the supervision of student safety is a discretionary function. Therefore, if school authorities managed their responsibility properly, the school officials would be entitled to immunity. In opposition, the lawyer for Caldwell argued that a state criminal statute against hazing transformed this discretionary policing function into a ministerial act; therefore the school officials did not have immunity in this circumstance. Caldwell's lawyer further argued that the coach and the principal each had a ministerial duty *not* to aid and abet their students in the criminal act of hazing, using the rationale that under Georgia law, school officials do not have the legal discretion to participate in a crime or to allow students under their supervision to commit a crime. Compliance with the law is mandatory, and in that sense arguably "ministerial."

Although the court found that the school had the responsibility to protect Caldwell, it found no evidence that the principal or the coach were parties to a crime or that they allowed a crime to occur. Thus the court did not support the ministerial duty argument. The court also held that neither the principal nor the coach acted with "actual malice" toward Caldwell. This is important because, if actual malice had been determined, the official immunity would not have protected the coach or the administrator from personal liability. Since the court found no evidence showing that either the coach or the principal had actively condoned, encouraged, or taken part in any of the initiation rites, or the violent attack on Caldwell, Caldwell's claim of actual malice must fail.

Negligence by the school or by a school employee often is an issue in high school hazing cases. For example, in *Bryant* v. *School Board of Duval County*, 399 So. 2d 417 (Fla. 1981), the court stated:

> By failing to carry out duty to execute and implement without negligence school board policy that no outing of student club could occur without permission of the school principal, and, if it occurred, it had to be attended by a faculty advisor, school board and its agents could be deemed negligent in that they would have permitted a chain of events to be set in motion which allegedly culminated in injury to student during club "hazing" at initiation ceremony unattended by faculty advisor.[23]

In this case, Glenn Bryant was paralyzed during an initiation ceremony of the Omega Club. Although the school had established rules forbidding hazing, club members hazed Bryant, severing his spinal cord in the process. Bryant unsuccessfully argued that the school was negligent. This case is important because it demonstrates that if a school board can prove that it established policies and regulations forbidding hazing prior to a hazing event, the school district may be able to avoid liability if a person is injured during a hazing activity.

Hazing cases have many similarities, but each also has its own distinctive aspects. For example, *Hilton* v. *Lincoln-Way High School*, No. 97-C-3872, 1998 WL 26174 (N.D. Ill. Jan. 14, 1998), contains a number of elements that distinguish it from other cases: the hazed individual was African-American, the plaintiff cited the wrong hazing statute while filing the paperwork of the case, Fourth and Fourteenth Amendment considerations surfaced, and the administrators alleged a lack of knowledge about the hazing. Lawyers for Hilton, a student, asserted various state law claims, including battery, false imprisonment, hazing, negligence, and intentional infliction of emotional distress. The case involved the initiation of Hilton and other students during band camp. Among the numerous allegations that surfaced during the trial, the court found sufficient evidence to support some, while rejecting others. For example, the court held that there was no evidence of a conspiracy against Hilton. The court did accept the relationship between the governmental agency, Lincoln-Way school, and Hilton in that when a government agency has taken someone into its care, they assume some level of responsibility. Interestingly, the arguments put forth by Hilton's attorney may actually have worked against him. Hilton's lawyer argued: "Lincoln-Way school officials at the highest level knew, or should have known, of those practices and those officials there by approved of them. Consequently, the retreat and its practice of hazing including Ku Klux Klan regalia and other rituals were official policy of defendant Lincoln-Way." The plaintiff's position was that the decision makers tacitly approved of the practices because they knew about, but remained silent about, the rituals. The argument that the school sanctioned the hazing activities probably worked against Hilton because Illinois hazing law delineated hazing as an activity *outside* the sanction of the education institution.

Finally, another type of tort action can arise if a party claims injury as a result of school officials acting in a manner that is *arbitrary or capricious*. When a decision is made — for example, to discipline hazers in a certain manner — using individual discretion, rather than depending on a fixed set of rules or procedures, or when a decision is based on prejudice or preference, rather than reason or fact, it is referred to as being "arbitrary and capricious."

In *McNaughton* v. *Circleville Board of Education*, 345 N.E. 2d 649 (Ohio 1974), the members of the Stooge Club held an initiation of new members off school property *without* notifying their advisor of the meeting. The principal suspended the students who actively took part in the initiation. A student then brought suit asking the court for a temporary and permanent order restraining and enjoining the defendant from enforcing the disciplinary action. The student's suit was based on the fact that school officials did not provide the student with the proper due process. The court found that the school official's actions were not arbitrary, unreasonable, or capricious. The court stated that "courts will not interfere with the exercise of discretion by school authorities, in the absence of an abuse of discretion or arbitrary, unreasonable or capricious action."[24] Because the principal's actions did not violate these standards, the court reaffirmed the school's right to suspend the students.

Defenses

Defendants in hazing cases typically resort to one or more of three basic defenses: 1) sovereign immunity or government immunity, 2) assumption of risk, and 3) contributory negligence.

Sovereign Immunity. The idea of sovereign immunity comes from the English concept that "the King can do no wrong."

American courts adopted this concept in the 1800s. Sovereign immunity protects a government agency from being sued in its own courts without its consent.[25] Most school districts are not "sovereign," and so protection under the concept of sovereign immunity usually is not available. However, if the legal action involves state funds, a school may qualify for protection under a concept related to sovereign immunity: government immunity. For most purposes, sovereign immunity and government immunity may be considered to be the same. Therefore, in some circumstances individuals may not sue a government entity such as a school board.

The principle behind government immunity is that the property and funds held by the government belong to all citizens. Money paid in a damage award to one citizen would be taken from funds intended to benefit all citizens. Therefore "all citizens" are protected through government immunity. But, in fact, a student who is injured may sue the school, in spite of the fact that it is a government entity, because recent changes in the law in many states have weakened the defense of government immunity. Three cases put this defense in perspective.

In *Sherwood* v. *Moxee School District No. 90*, 363 P.2d 138 (Wash. 1961), the school district asked the court to address the question of sovereign immunity and whether the Sherwoods had the right to sue the school district for negligence. The Sherwoods sued the Moxee School District after the death of their son, who was a student at Moxee High School. The parents alleged that their son died during an initiation ceremony of a high school varsity athletes' society. The complaint claimed that the initiation in question was conducted under the auspices and supervision of school district employees and that the tragedy was the result of their negligence. In this case, the court referred to an act of the territorial legislature of 1869, which indicated school districts are vicariously liable for negligence. The court went on to say that many judges, courts, and writers erroneously believe that, by the common law of England, school districts are not liable for negligence because of sovereign immunity. However, this is incorrect; schools always have been vicariously liable for negligence.

In *S.W. and J.W.* v. *Spring Lake Park School District No. 16*, 566 N.W.2d 366 (Minn. 1997), the state supreme court considered whether a government entity is entitled to official immunity when a public official claims entitlement to official immunity. This case explored the issue of the school district's responsibility to provide students with a safe and secure environment. The controversy arose after a nonschool employee brutally, sexually attacked a 15-year-old student during school hours. The court stated that in order to determine entitlement to immunity, one must look at the action, or inaction, of the challenged public official. Only if the public official is entitled to official immunity will the government entity be entitled to vicarious official immunity. In this case, the court found that the employees were not entitled to official immunity, and thus the district was not entitled to vicarious official immunity. In order to make this determination, the court reviewed whether the employees' actions were discretionary or ministerial in nature. Suits dealing with immunity represent a clash of interests: the right to sue a public entity over some alleged failure to provide care versus the legislature's intent to protect that same public entity from large monetary damages.

In *Ledfors* v. *Emery County School District*, 849 P.2d 1162 (Utah 1993), the court considered claims involving assault, liability, and governmental immunity. This case arose after a student reported to the building principal that several students had repeatedly attacked him. The principal assured the student that he would take care of the problem. About a month later, two students attacked the student while he was in a classroom left unsupervised by a teacher. The court held that the school was protected from liability by the doctrine of government immunity. The court also stated:

> In reaching this decision, we are sympathetic to Richie's [attacked student] plight. It is unfortunate that any parent who is required by state law to send his or her child to school lacks a civil remedy against negligent school personnel who fail to assure the child's safety at school. Nevertheless, the legislature has spoken with clarity on the question

of immunity, and we are constrained by the plain language of the Act and our prior case law on this point. However, as we stated in *O'Neal v. Division of Family Services,* "Certainly, the legislature is not so constrained as we." 821 P.2d 1139, 1145 (Utah 1991). It is entirely within the legislature's power to permit all plaintiffs to whom the government owes a duty of care based on a special relationship to sue for injuries arising out of a breach of that duty. Alternatively, the legislature could tailor the waiver of immunity more narrowly; the state could permit suit by or on behalf of public school children injured because of such a breach of duty. Its power to craft waivers of immunity is far superior to ours.[26]

The court suggested that immunity would not be appropriate if a school had breached the duty owed to schoolchildren. However, the laws of Utah in place at the time of the incident supported the school; therefore the case was dismissed.

Assumption of Risk. The fact that a victim voluntarily participated in a hazing incident has long been used as a basic defense strategy. Courts have ruled that the doctrine of "assumption of risk" has merit as an affirmative defense in hazing cases in which the individual consented to participate and was, therefore, responsible for his or her own injury. In order to determine the validity of this defense, courts must evaluate two questions: Did the plaintiff know of and appreciate the danger or risk involved? Did the plaintiff voluntarily consent to expose himself or herself to the danger?

The underlying notion here is that people do not volunteer to be harmed. Thus, if a person knowingly and voluntarily risks danger, he or she cannot recover damages for any resulting injury — in principle. Assumption of risk means that a person expressly relieves another person of responsibility for his or her safety. But assumption of risk is not absolute.

Following is an illustration of the assumption of risk principle: A young man signs up for the football team, attends all the practices, and then, during the first game, is injured. The boy claims that the football game was too rough and that the school placed him in danger by allowing him to participate in this game. The school district's defense would cite assumption of risk. The student knew the dangers inherent in playing football and accepted them by staying on the team. Would the defense be successful? Not necessarily. This is essentially the same defense used in the 1940s *DeGooyer* case, cited earlier in this chapter, in which the student knew of the hazing tradition and accepted responsibility by willingly participating in the activity that subsequently proved fatal. The court agreed with the school district defendants that the evidence indicated that Gerald DeGooyer knew that the hazing events would include being shocked. Yes, the boy had assumed risk. But the court judged the athletic director to have been negligent for not safeguarding DeGooyer.

Another decision may shine some light on the reasoning of the court. *Siesto* v. *Bethpage Union Free School District, QDS,* 72701944 (Nassau County Sup. Ct. N.Y. 1999) also addressed the defense of assumption of risk. In this case, the student argued that he endured an injury during a traditional hazing ritual in which veteran players wearing weighted pads hit the younger players. As a defense, the attorneys for the school district asserted that the student knew of the hazing rituals and assumed the risk when he agreed to be part of the team. The court disagreed:

> While a student athlete assumes the risk of injury inherent in the sport in which he or she participates, such student does not assume the risk of injury from a hazing ritual or tradition, which has no place in organized student athletics, even if they have knowledge that such rituals or traditions exist.[27]

By way of contrast, *Jones v. Kent,* 35 A.D.2d 622 (N.Y. 1970), a non-hazing case, addressed a situation in which a student plaintiff voluntarily and knowingly accepted a challenge to meet another boy between classes in order to engage in a fight. Both students were members of the same social studies class. The students agreed to meet in an area near the restroom after class. The court said the student clearly did not use good judgment in this situation because he had time after class to change his mind about the meeting, but he elected to walk from class to the agreed location in order to fight. Therefore the student assumed the risk and was not entitled to compensation for injuries he suffered during the fight.

Contributory Negligence. One "contributes" to an injury by willingly participating in the act that causes the injury. Some hazers have argued that once an individual allows others to haze him, he releases the hazers from liability. Most courts have rejected this defense. However, as the next case illustrates, the court may determine a hazed youth contributed to his own injury under certain circumstances.

In *Harden* v. *United States*, 688 F.2d 1025 (5th Cir. 1982), the parents of 15-year-old Clay Harden sued for the wrongful death of their son. The family brought suit after a camp ranger shot Clay on the campground for which the ranger was responsible. The tragedy occurred during a hazing incident that got out of control. After a non-jury trial, the district court found that the ranger, an employee of the government, was negligent — but that Clay Harden also was negligent. The court concluded that Harden's own negligence contributed to his injury to the extent of 25%, with the resulting award reduced by that percentage.

The preceding descriptions illustrate the various defenses and some of the many interpretations that the court can make based on the merits of individual cases. *Harden* includes, along with an example of the contributory negligence defense, one type of remedy.

Remedies

A remedy is the means by which an injured party attempts to secure redress for an alleged violation of a law. Remedies for hazing cases usually fall into two categories: criminal prosecution or civil suit for damages. Criminal prosecution occurs when a person is charged with violating a criminal law. A civil suit would be one person filing a civil complaint against another and seeking a monetary award. Both criminal and civil remedies can and often do occur within the same case.

Criminal Prosecution. This first example of a criminal prosecution involves a death that occurred during a hazing activity. *Lester Brannon* v. *State*, 217 P. 1060 (Okla. Ct. App. 1923) is an appeal of the conviction of Lester Brannon, a 16-year-old male, who was charged with the manslaughter death of Claude Wilson. The victim and some 20 to 25 other males surrounded Brannon and another young male. These youths hazed Brannon, tearing his clothes, slapping him, and beating him. At some point Wilson punched Brannon. In response Brannon stabbed Wilson. Although Wilson received medical care and appeared to be on the way to recovery, an infection set in. Two months after the stabbing, Wilson died. The court found Brannon guilty of manslaughter and sentenced him to the state reformatory for two years.

In *People* v. *Lenti*, 46 Misc. 2d 682, 682 (N.Y.S. 1965), authorities brought criminal charges against Robert Lenti and others for hazing fraternity pledges. Because of the ambiguous wording of the New York hazing statute, which states, in part, "and whoever participates in the same shall be deemed guilty of a misdemeanor," the court dismissed all charges. The court opined that "participants" must include the pledges, the individuals for whom the legislature enacted this statute; but because the statute was so vague, the court could have interpreted it to mean that the pledges also were guilty of violating the laws initially designed to protect them from actions of others.

Criminal cases involving hazing can happen anywhere in any given year. Following are three examples from 2000:

In Arizona a Winslow High School coach faced felony charges of child endangering after a sexual hazing occurred at school. Eight athletes attacked underclassmen, held them down, and inserted pencils, markers, and fingers into the younger students' rectums. Some of the attacks took place on a bus trip after a basketball game. Several victims leveled charges against the attackers that included sexual assault and kidnapping.[28]

At Wolcott High School in Connecticut, administrators suspended six starting football players after these players beat three freshmen players with a plastic baseball bat during a hazing incident. Several of the players faced adult charges of second-degree unlawful restraint and conspiracy to commit third-degree assault.[29]

Mount Zion High School officials in Illinois dealt with a high school hazing incident in which students beat two junior high school students during a hazing activity that included paddling. Two of the paddlings happened on school property, while two occurred elsewhere. In Illinois, hazing is a Class A misdemeanor that carries a possible penalty of up to one year in jail.[30]

Civil Suit. In cases involving civil remedies, the plaintiff seeks a monetary award. Monetary awards are variously made for purposes of equity, as compensation for tangible losses (such as payment of medical bills), as compensation for intangible losses (such as humiliation), or as punishment of the guilty party. Following is an example:

In a well-publicized hazing case, *Seamons* v. *Snow*, 864 F.Supp. 1111, (N.D. Utah 1994), *app.*, 206 F.3d 1021, the victim sued the school district and the coach. Brian Seamons sued the coach both as an individual and in his capacity as coach. In this case, Seamons, a high school football player, was tied naked to a horizontal towel bar and his former girlfriend was paraded in front of him. After the hazing allegations surfaced, the principal cancelled a football playoff game. The student body viewed Seamons as the cause of the game cancellation, thus creating a "hostile environment" in which his classmates threatened and harassed Seamons. Seamons sued, alleging violations of Title IX, his First Amendment right to free speech, and conspiracy. After two district court decisions and two appeals to the Tenth Circuit, Seamons was awarded $250,000 for the coach's violation of Seamons' First Amendment right to free speech. This award arose because the court determined that school officials attempted to stop the student from discussing the hazing case with members of the media.

Multiple Issues

Some cases that begin over hazing incidents are expanded to address larger legal issues. For example, in *Poway Unified School District* v. *Superior Court of Appeal,* 1998.CA.333 (Ca. 1998), the court explored a student's right to privacy. In this case, three 16-year-old sophomores used a broomstick to brutally sodomize a 15-year-old freshman in the Poway Unified School District. After a court hearing, reporters from the *Union-Tribune* (San Diego) publicized the hazing story in the newspaper. The newspaper did not publicize the name of the victim or the perpetrators; but later the *Union-Tribune*, owned by Copley Press, sought access "to any and all claims filed with the school district between March 20, 1997 through July 18, 1997" as permitted under the Public Records Act. The superior court ordered the settlement sealed, and the school district refused to provide information about the unresolved claims. Then Copley Press filed a petition contending that the reason provided for nondisclosure did not apply; thereafter the court ruled in favor of Copley Press. Poway School District complied with the court order and released all appropriate records. However, the school district later filed a petition with the court requesting written guidelines clarifying their legal responsibility with regard to the release of records. In response to this petition, the court explained the following legal concepts: 1) what constitutes a public record, 2) the public's need to be informed regarding the actions of government, 3) the public's right to know versus the victim's right to privacy, 4) the state's interest in protecting the privacy of sex offense victims, and 5) privacy as one of the California Constitution's inalienable rights.

If one were to select a single high school hazing case to study, the civil case, *Rupp* v. *School Board of Duval County*, 417 So. 2d 658 (Fla.1982), should be that case. *Rupp* has been cited in almost every hazing lawsuit since 1981. This case involves most of the elements discussed in this chapter and clearly illustrates how all of the legal pieces fit together. In this case, the parents of a boy who was paralyzed after a hazing incident argued that the principal and the teacher were 100% liable. The principal and the teacher, to the contrary, claimed immunity. In order to determine whether the principal and the teacher could be held personally liable, the court needed to determine if they owed the boy, Glenn Bryant, a special duty of care and if the injury occurred in the course of the principal's and teacher's ministerial care. The court refined "special duty" to include the term "special damages."

Sovereign (government) immunity was one of the issues examined by the *Rupp* court. The Supreme Court of Florida had to determine if a district court's decision to declare Florida's sovereign immunity statute unconstitutional was appropriate. In this case, the court was looking at the Laws of Florida number 768.28, which states:

> No officer, employee, or agent of the state or its subdivisions shall be held personally liable in tort or named as a party defendant in any action for a final judgment which has been rendered against him for any injuries or damages suffered as a result of any act, event, or omission of action in the scope of his employment or function, unless such officer, employee, or agent acted in bad faith or with malicious purpose or in manner exhibiting wanton and willful disregard of human rights, safety, or property. . . . The state or its officer, employee, or agent shall not be liable in tort for the acts or omissions of an officer, employee, or agent committed while acting outside the course and scope of his employment or committed in bad faith or with malicious purpose or in a manner exhibiting wanton and willful disregard of human rights, safety, or property.[31]

The court determined that the injuries sustained by Bryant unquestionably met the "special damages" prong of the test. In order to determine whether the other prong, ministerial care, was met, the court needed to decide whether the teacher and the principal's duty to supervise Bryant was ministerial or discretionary in nature. In making this determination, the court looked to other jurisdictions for guidance. The court found that many courts had confronted this same issue and had determined that this duty to supervise was a ministerial duty, not a discretionary one. Thus the court held that the teacher and the principal could not use immunity as a defense.

The court then looked at the factors involved in the case. Regarding whether the school owed a duty to Bryant, the court held that it did. Because a duty had been established, the court examined the facts to find out if there had been a breach of that duty. In addition, this determination included establishing whether the breach, if found, was the proximate cause of the injury. Further, the court had to determine whether the breach of duty was a foreseeable consequence of the school's failure to supervise the students. The court clearly established its position by stating:

> Under the facts of this case, there can be little doubt that accidents of this type are foreseeably the result of absence of supervision. This conclusion is reinforced by the school board's own prohibition of hazing and requirements of the principal's approval of outings and the teacher's attendance at all meetings. Not only was this harm foreseeable, but also the school had actually anticipated it through regulations, which it failed to follow. The errant reputation of the Omega Club bespoke its unreliability and need for supervision.[32]

The last issue the court addressed was the allegation that the teacher and the principal acted with personal, "wanton and willful," negligence. The standards used to determine gross negligence are actions or omissions that rise to the level of reckless disregard of human life or rights, which in turn is the equivalent to an intentional act or conscious indifference to the consequences of an act. The court held that neither the teacher's nor the principal's actions rose to that level.

These two important determinations are key. First, the teacher and the principal were not entitled to official immunity. However, the court found that their actions did not constitute behavior that the court considered wanton and willful. Second, the principal and the teacher were responsible for the injuries to Bryant, though not because the school employees intentionally did things to harm the student.

In summary, the reality is that most hazing cases — indeed, most legal cases — resemble *Rupp* in the sense that they are complex and involve multiple issues that the court must address. Although we have singled out some examples to illustrate the various types of tort actions, defenses, and remedies, most of these examples are more complex than may be apparent from the short summaries provided here.

Responsibilities of School Authorities

School authorities have a legal duty to care for the children under their charge. Those responsible for the care of children include the teacher or coach directly assigned to the class or activity, the building administrators, the athletic director, the principal, the central office administrators, the board of education, the parents of the hazers, and the hazers themselves.

Generally, the teacher or coach has direct responsibility for the supervision of the students under his or her care. Supervisors are the ones best able to maintain the "pulse" of the group and determine if any proverbial red flags are waving. If a supervisor demonstrates vigilance, this may be enough to stop a hazing from occurring in the first place. If the authority figure is alert to signs of distress by the students, acting on those signs may limit any potential legal exposure. While a teacher or coach assumes responsibility for the well-being of his students, this does not automatically mean he or she is negligent if a hazing event occurs while he or she is in charge. Courts generally will hold these individuals accountable only if the accuser can prove that the teacher or coach was negligent in some manner.

A building-level administrator's legal exposure is different from that of a teacher or coach. Courts will look at the administrator as being the one who knew, or should have known, of the potential for hazing to occur. The building-level administrator is responsible for all actions of employees under supervision. Thus, if negligence is established at the teacher level, the courts will look for a nexus between the teacher's action and the building administrator. The principal may limit his or her exposure to liability by making sure that hazing policies are in place and that employees are aware of the policies.

In addition, the building administrator assumes another type of liability: the potential for lawsuits from those suspended due to the hazing incident. Courts will carefully scrutinize the actions taken by the building administrator. Therefore an accurate analysis of the situation is important. The court will want to know if all the procedures were followed in a timely fashion. The court also will look to see if there were nuances of board policy that the building administrator skipped or performed in an incorrect manner or order. If hazing has been a tradition and the principal was unaware of it, then the court will want to know how many other activities have occurred without his knowledge.

Another problem for the building administrator arises when the administrator must take action to discipline the teacher or coach involved. In this case, the administrator is open to accusations of not being supportive of the teaching staff. On the other hand, if the administrator takes no action, then this may set a tone that the administrator condones hazing.

The superintendent represents the district. Although responsible to the school board for employees' actions or inactions, there should be a degree of separation from the position and the hazing event. If at all possible, depending on the extent of the anger, disgust, or mistrust due to the hazing incident, the school superintendent should allow the building-level administrator to resolve the problem internally. However, when concerns escalate to the level where attorneys are involved and lawsuits are being filed or considered, the superintendent's involvement obviously increases. The superintendent may be able to limit the liability of the school district by being politically astute, as well as empathic toward the hazed students and the parents of those involved. By listening and attempting to solve problems, the superintendent may "keep a lid" on the incident and, more important, resolve it before it escalates.

When someone sues a district, obviously the board of education is involved. Although the board of education, as an entity, may have some degree of governmental immunity, this is not full immunity. The board will have to expend resources defending itself, whether or not a jury or judge later determines that the board is entitled to governmental immunity. Another consideration is that the cost of continuing the legal battle sometimes exceeds the potential cost of settlement. On the other hand, while a settlement may be less costly, it can make the district appear guilty. This can present a potentially difficult situation. Furthermore, when negative things happen in a school district, the issues, concerns, and frustrations associated with that situation affect each individual board member.

In 1996 police in Texas investigated how much adults from Perryton High School knew of a hazing situation involving a football player. A 15-year-old student had Icy Hot rubbed on his skin and genitals after he entered the varsity locker room. The teens faced Class A misdemeanor charges of assault with intent to cause bodily injury. The teens faced a maximum punishment of $4,000 in fines and one year in jail. The judge acquitted two teens and, after two other students pleaded no contest to charges of assault, he gave them 40 hours of community service. The parents of the hazed student filed a federal lawsuit against the district alleging that it failed to stop hazing at Perryton High School.[33]

Sometimes, the hazing cycle is broken or halted, and therefore the potential for injury and liability decreases. The school authority that is diligent in its supervision and handles rumors of hazing activities may interrupt the cycle of hazing.

The Costs of Hazing

It may be useful to look at what hazing costs school districts from several vantage points. One vantage point simply is money.

Assume that the district is found to be negligent and ends up paying $150,000 for the settlement and related legal fees. Regardless of whether this amount is awarded by the court or negotiated in an out-of-court settlement, it is a significant sum. It is equivalent to perhaps three teachers' annual salaries or, in some districts, the cost of all the textbooks for a given subject. Added to this amount, of course, arc the "hidden" costs of work time spent on investigating the hazing incident and attending to legal matters, instead of in the classroom or the administrative office.

Some school districts have insurance coverage to deflect the financial effect of a settlement, but such coverage may be conditional and should not be taken for granted. It would be prudent for school districts to consider the costs and benefits of such insurance protection.

Finally, there is an emotional cost. Hazing incidents, resulting injuries, and legal battles are personally stressful for those directly involved. There also are indirect effects on friends and families of all of the individuals. Tarnished reputations can affect the future lives of the students — both hazers and victims — and of school officials. A rift between the school and the community can be opened by a hazing event that goes awry.

All of these factors must be considered in weighing the costs of hazing. Taken together, they offer a compelling reason for schools to address the problem of hazing and work toward its elimination.

CHAPTER THREE

Assessing Local Issues

Over time, hazing has been transformed from a rite of passage to something substantially different. Rites, as defined by the traditions of fraternal organizations, once consisted mainly of oaths, pledges, and commitments made to the organization. These rites were, in a sense, like marriage rites, binding the initiate to the group. They were pledges of loyalty.

Loyalty to a group increases as the newcomer comes closer to the inner circle. That loyalty is bolstered by heightened commitment and increased feelings of closeness. The more the newcomer bonds with other loyal members, the more he or she becomes one with the group.

Hazing is a physical manifestation of the loyalty rite, often a bonding through pain. Inflicting pain and receiving pain are forms of intimacy that enhance the bond between individuals and between the initiate and the group. When pain comes in the form of sexual abuse, intimacy can be further heightened.

It can be argued that hazing activities mirror the mores of society. As society has become increasingly violent, some observers aver, so has hazing. The physical and sexual punishments associated with hazing once were visited only on males, but now female groups engage in some of the same behaviors. But so, too, has society's repugnance at violent behavior increased. Activities that once were put down as "horseplay" or "boys being boys" are now actionable. The paddling that once was the price of admission can now be grounds for a lawsuit. Hazing, even in fairly mild forms, is no longer something toward which authorities can afford to turn a blind eye.

A hazing incident at McAteer High School in the San Francisco area provides an example. A 17-year-old student suffered a seriously lacerated scrotum when a broom handle slipped as older students were poking him during a hazing incident. The school principal suspended the hazers and then was himself suspended by the superintendent for improperly handling the incident. When the information surfaced, the community was outraged to learn that such hazing practices had been going on for at least four years prior to the incident in which the student was seriously injured.[34]

Hazing and School Climate

A tradition of hazing cannot flourish without a climate that supports it. Although most schools do not actively support hazing as part of any initiation ritual, many schools provide passive support simply by not challenging the existence of hazing.

When a hazing incident results in legal action, the court usually looks not only at the specifics of the incident — who participated, who was injured, etc. — but also at the climate of the institution or community in which the hazing took place. For example, what patterns of behavior might have warned school officials about the possibility of hazing? Why were these warning signs overlooked? What institutional attitudes permitted (or perhaps tacitly encouraged) the hazing?

If schools are serious about halting hazing activities, school authorities first must take a hard look at the climate for hazing in their schools and then set about addressing what they find. The most productive stance is one that is proactive, rather than reactive. It is better to have policies in place that forbid hazing and to implement practices that actively discourage hazers than to formulate policies and practices after a hazing incident has resulted in a student's injury or death.

The community that surrounds the institution also must be part of the solution to the hazing problem. Fostering an anti-hazing stance within the institution will not succeed if hazing still is sanctioned in other contexts. Also, if hazing activities have always been fairly innocuous, they will be more difficult to eradicate. Initiates to a farming group may see nothing wrong with getting their hands painted green, for example. But it should not take a case of paint toxicity resulting in serious illness or death to discourage this seemingly mild form of hazing. Hazing of all types is better extinguished on principle — before someone is hurt.

In examining the potential for hazing, school and community officials also do well to consider contexts in which hazing might occur. For example, many football teams conduct hazing activities related to the sport. Students may be hazed by being put to physical tests in the locker room or on the playing field. These are contexts and locations where school officials must be watchful. Situations in which supervision may be limited, such as sports or music camps, often are used for hazing activities. The elimination of hazing in these contexts may require added supervision or the restriction of some activities if such supervision is unavailable.

As we discussed in the previous chapter, institutions place themselves in financial peril by allowing hazing to occur, especially after becoming aware of such practices. *Sovereign Camp, W.O.W.*, 170 So. 634; *Rupp*, 417 So. 2d 658; and *DeGooyer*, 13 N.W.2d 816, are examples of cases where the court looked at the climate of hazing traditions.

Individual school employees also risk their jobs when they permit hazing. An incident at Toms River High School in New Jersey can serve as an example. School employees allowed an eight-year hazing tradition to continue because no one complained. Then, after a 1981 hazing incident, which involved freshmen being humiliated in a rite nicknamed "Freshman Kill Day," parents spoke out about their concerns with the traditional ceremony. The ceremony consisted of freshmen running a gauntlet of seniors who kicked, hit, punched, and used fire hoses on the freshmen. At this point, the school authorities dismissed three soccer coaches for permitting the hazing to go on.[35]

Speaking Up

Speaking up is a way to help change a school's climate from one that condones hazing to one that condemns it. This is true for school officials, but it is equally true for students and former students. Not all who are hazed become hazers themselves. Some become strong anti-hazing advocates.

"Owning the problem" is a well-known strategy for initiating attitudinal change. School officials will not be able to eradicate hazing unless they first change their own and others' perception that hazing is someone else's problem. Often students and graduates who have endured hazing can be powerful allies of school officials seeking to change school climate. Some of these individuals have spoken up at the national level. Following are a few examples:

- Hank Nuwer is the author of several books dealing with hazing, including *High School Hazing: When Rites Become Wrongs* (Franklin Watts, 2000).
- Brian Rahill is the webmaster for a Stop Hazing site on the Internet (www.stophazing.org), devoted to eliminating hazing through education.
- Lizzie Murtie, an activist, successfully lobbied for passage of an anti-hazing law in Vermont.
- Eileen Stevens founded the Committee to Halt Useless College Killings, or C.H.U.C.K (c/o Eileen Stevens, P.O. Box 188, Sayville, NY 11782).

Actress Nikki Costentino (*Grumpier Old Men*) became an anti-hazing activist because of an incident in which she was involved in 1995. Costentino, then a student at Roseville High School in Minnesota, was party to a hazing incident in which alcohol was a factor. As many as 100 senior hazers allegedly overpowered male and female sophomores, breaking bottles over the heads of some students.[36]

Every school that has hazing has hazing survivors, whether they are individuals who were hazed, who did the hazing, or both.

These individuals are well positioned to speak out against hazing. By so doing, they can help school officials break the cycle of hazing and change the school climate so that future hazing is not condoned.

Legal Grounds and Responsibility

States laws on hazing vary widely. School officials need to find out what the applicable laws are in their state and local community. Tables (see Appendix A) are provided to show basic legal provisions in the states. These provisions may be modified or supplemented by specific local laws and policies. Hazing is a serious and controversial matter, so it would not be out of place for school officials to become familiar with applicable case law.

The next step is for school officials to ensure that district and school policies are consistent with the applicable laws. However, in some cases, taking this next step will require developing policies, a subject that we take up in the next chapter.

Law and policy matters address hazing at the formal level. At the informal level, eliminating hazing requires school officials to take personal responsibility. When the principal of a 1,400-student high school says that hazing is "under control" because only 56 football players were involved in a hazing incident, that principal is not taking full responsibility for the problem of hazing. Hazing cannot be minimized by reducing an incident to a statistic, by calling it "horseplay," or by shrugging off the activities of hazers as merely "tradition."

Taking personal responsibility means that school officials must take reports of hazing seriously and investigate all allegations of hazing — even when those allegations come weeks or months after the alleged hazing event. It is not unusual for hazing victims to be slow to come to terms with their experience and to realize that it is all right to seek redress. Attending to allegations of past hazing can help school officials send a message that they are serious about eradicating hazing. Doing otherwise sends a message that hazing is condoned.

Another issue in taking responsibility is being open and honest. Too often hazing incidents are covered up, sometimes in a misguided attempt to save embarrassment to the school or district, to school administrators, to the hazers or their victims, and so on. Whenever such cover-ups come to light, the level of embarrassment is even higher. Moreover, cover-ups also send a message that hazing is not serious enough to confront head-on; it can be swept under the carpet and ignored. The problem is even worse when school officials abet the hazers. A case in point: At Shoshone High School in Idaho, it was alleged in 1994 that school administrators operated a lottery to match hazers and victims.[37]

Drawing the Line

Competition and friendly rivalry are part of the school experience. But it is necessary to draw a line between normal class competition (for example, seniors versus juniors raising funds for a school project) and negative competition for physical or psychological dominance that can lead to hazing and the acceptance of hazing. School officials need to be wary about crossing this line.

A class competition — who can cheer loudest at a pep rally — may pit older students against their younger peers. The message may be translated: It's us (upperclassmen) against the freshmen. And that can set the stage for older students hazing younger students. Another potential problem is physical competition pitting older, stronger students against younger, weaker peers. When "might makes right" is sanctioned, hazing may follow on the same basis.

When the line between competition and hazing is blurred, teachers, coaches, and other school officials may fail to see an incident as hazing simply because they have not learned to discern the distinguishing characteristics. A hazing incident may be reported but interpreted as something else. For example, when a student scratches an obscene word or picture on another student's locker, is the victim an individual target? Or is the incident related to the offender attempting to assert dominance on behalf of his or her group over the victim? The first interpretation is not hazing; the second is. But it may take repeated incidents of this sort for school officials to discern a pattern and then define the incidents as hazing.

In considering the climate of a school and the potential for hazing, school administrators do well to think about several questions:

- Are there longstanding traditions of hazing by particular groups? Who is knowledgeable about hazing incidents? Do the responsible adults support, or tacitly support, hazing?
- When students inform school authorities of a hazing situation, what has been the response? Was the response effective? If so, what made the response effective? If not, are changes possible that would make the response effective?
- Are there unsupervised activities by certain groups? How do students spread the word about unstructured or unsupervised events or activities?
- Is there adult supervision in locker rooms? Do school authorities keep the locker rooms locked at those times when no one is supposed to be in them?

These and similar questions need to be considered as school authorities review the climate of their schools.

Finally, it is important to include *all* key personnel in the work to eradicate hazing. School custodians should not be overlooked. Custodians can be trained to look for "typical" potential evidence of hazing. Potential evidence may include shaving cream wiped on lockers or duct tape with hair on the adhesive side thrown in the trash baskets. Do custodians find empty food containers, such as mustard or pickle jars or hot sauce bottles, in unusual locations? Suspicious materials should be reported.

CHAPTER FOUR

Taking Action

The following discussion focuses on the specific steps that school authorities can take to reduce hazing in their schools.

Formulating Policies on Hazing

A prerequisite for controlling or stopping hazing is to develop and disseminate a policy regarding hazing. When developing such a policy, the logical place to start is with the current state laws. For example, Pennsylvania had a statewide initiative; the Pennsylvania School Boards Association sent out a draft of a policy statement to about 350 members of the association with the hope that boards of education would adopt the policy. The association drafted this policy using the state's hazing law as its philosophical basis.

Any policy that is developed needs to be broad enough to cover the spectrum of hazing activities but not so broad as to be ambiguous. A hazing policy should include a definition of hazing as it is defined by the state's hazing statute. If the state does not have a hazing statute, legal advice for an appropriate definition should be sought. The policy also should include a statement that covers hazing activities both on and off school property, and it should make clear that school-owned property includes both buildings and vehicles. In addition, the hazing policy should include a statement that, if administrators learn of a hazing situation, they will notify in a timely fashion the parents of both the hazers and the individuals who were hazed.

Once the board of education has adopted the policy, the next step should be the dissemination of the information. Communication must be open to the entire student body, not just to those suspected of participating in hazing activities. The hazing policy should be included in the school and district handbooks so that it is available to every student. It also should be posted in conspicuous locations, such as locker rooms and hallways. Administrators should provide inservice training to staff about the potential liability that they and the district would face if they allow student hazing to occur.

School personnel need to review the policies and procedures adopted by organizations to ascertain if the group has taken an official stance against hazing. Students in various organizations have the ability to make the decision to halt hazing activities. However, some students in a position to determine whether to continue the tradition of hazing face a dilemma. As underclassmen, they felt humiliated and demeaned. Some want to stop the traditions, while others want the opportunity to continue the process. It is critical to find those student leaders who want to stop hazing and to enlist their help in making it happen.

Many states have laws governing college hazing incidents but do not address the hazing activities of high school students. In order to help minimize the number of high school students hazed each year, advocating for the passage of a strong hazing statutes in all states is appropriate. While passage of a hazing statute will not directly reduce the number of high school hazing cases, at least it will ensure that those injured have legal remedies.

Articulating Expectations for Supervision

Adults in leadership positions are responsible for student behavior. Not everyone may understand or accept that seemingly obvious fact. Therefore the responsible administrator should articulate the expectation to principals, coaches, teachers, and other adults that they will be responsible for student behavior and that this responsibility will be part of their performance evaluation. This understanding will set the tone that the adult is in charge and that the school administration expects him or her to remain in charge.

While the intent is to eliminate hazing, school districts also must focus on minimizing their exposure to liability. In order to accomplish both goals, the principal or other individual in charge must clearly communicate expectations for supervision. Failure to establish and articulate such expectations may increase a district's liability. For example, teachers must understand that providing proper and consistent supervision of students is a job standard. This expectation of supervisory vigilance is heightened whenever the potential for hazing incidents is high, such as on trips, especially when they involve overnight stays. Examples include band camps and summer sports camps.

Ensuring that policies are provided in writing and obtaining proof (signatures) that students and parents have seen the rules and expectations will allow staff to make a stronger case for prudent supervision should a hazing incident occur in spite of precautions.

Enforcing Hazing Policies

Swift enforcement of the hazing policy whenever violations occur will send the message that hazing is not an accepted activity. This may mean suspending students from activities or even from school.

A caution is necessary. There have been numerous cases in which students who were suspended for hazing later sued for restitution. These students claimed that they suffered damages because of the improper suspension. Therefore a district must ensure that proper procedures are followed in terms of due process. Part of this process is keeping records.

Maintaining accurate records of actions taken to prevent or respond to a hazing incident is important for two reasons. First, good recordkeeping can decrease the school's exposure to liability. Second, it can assist in interrupting the cycle of hazing. A record could be as simple as a description of the hazing incident and the individuals involved and a log of actions taken by school authorities regarding the incident. The court will look at the date when the hazing policy was established and whether policy information was properly disseminated. The court also will consider whether prior complaints were brought to the administrator's attention and whether those complaints were dealt with in a timely and appropriate manner. In attempting to interrupt the cycle of hazing, it often is possible to anticipate hazing in certain circumstances by reviewing collected information.

The strongest message against hazing comes from civil lawsuits. Damage awards run into the millions. The financial and emotional costs of defending a teacher or a coach can be debilitating. Having accurate records and a paper trail of actions taken will assist in preparing a defense if a parent files charges against a school system, a school, or an individual.

CONCLUSION

Psychologists have recognized that people will go to great lengths to be accepted by their peers. This need for acceptance may prevent a student from interfering in the hazing of another student. Or a student may not offer to help because he or she fears the hazer. And the hazed student who seeks to belong to the group also will remain silent — and may later haze others in the perpetuation of tradition.

At Essex High School in Vermont, Lizzie Murtie kept silent about a simulated sex act during a hazing incident. She maintained her silence for many months until another parent heard the story and spoke to Lizzie's parents. In the meantime, Lizzie's grades had fallen and she felt miserable throughout the year. Yet she remained silent. As the hazing incident became known, Lizzie is reported to have broken down crying and saying to her parents, "I can finally tell you."[38] Lizzie Murtie and her mother, Linda, became advocates of anti-hazing legislation in Vermont and were successful in lobbying for an anti-hazing bill.

A nationally publicized hazing case involving the hockey team from the University of Vermont aided the Murties in their drive to have the bill passed. Students on the hockey team lied about the hazing incident in order to protect other team members involved in the hazing incident. Once the administration realized that the students had lied to them, school officials canceled the hockey season.

Art Taylor, a psychologist at the Center for the Study of Sport in Society at Northeastern University in Massachusetts, believes that those who support the contention that hazing forms strong bonds among team members are fooling themselves. He suggests that humiliating hazing activities are likely to tear groups apart. He goes on to say that the students who enjoy hazing others in brutal or humiliating ways are more likely than nonhazers to become abusive to their spouses or their children.[39]

The phrase "code of silence" is applicable in situations where students and others within the school community know about hazing policy violations but refuse to disclose this information to authorities. In *McNaughton* v. *Circleville Board of Education,* allegations surfaced that the conditions that promoted and condoned hazing existed because neither parents nor students informed school authorities of hazing incidents that were known to them. After an administrator disciplined several students for their participation in hazing, the students and parents alleged that the school knew and approved of these activities. The *McNaughton* court stated:

> This presents a case that is more often true in some homes than at school, namely that within the school community everyone but the school officials seemed to know what was going on. As usual, this condition existed because neither parents nor the student wished to inform the school authorities of the facts. Greater surveillance, supervision, and cooperation are required of the school and parents involved.[40]

Teachers and administrators need to know about a problem in order to have the opportunity to correct it. Unfortunately, they often are not notified until it is too late. It is not until a problem surfaces that school officials learn that the activity had been going on for some time.

Thus it is important for school officials to take a proactive stance. Many high schools are working to replace hazing traditions with "helping traditions." Helping activities take many forms. Some examples include revamped freshman orientation strategies and school and community involvement, ranging from school clean-up days to senior citizen help weeks. The purpose of these activities is to instill in students a sense of camaraderie built not on trial and humiliation, as hazing is, but on bonding through shared activities that benefit themselves and others.

Not everyone will accept the new helping traditions at once. To eliminate hazing, school administrators will need to be persistent and to involve parents, students, and other community members in changing traditions. Over time, such efforts will pay off. Hazing can be eliminated when there is a collective assertion of will and a strong effort to do so.

NOTES

1. Fraternity Insurance Purchasing Group, "FIPG Risk Management Manual" (December 2003). www.fipg.org/media/FIPGRiskMgmt Manual.pdf
2. Nadine C. Hoover and Norman J. Pollard, *Initiation Rites in American High Schools: A National Survey's Final Report* (Alfred, N.Y.: Alfred University, 2000).
3. *Hilton v. Lincoln-Way High School*, No. 97-C-3872, 1998 WL 26174 (N.D. Ill. Jan. 14, 1998).
4. Karen Guzman, "School Board Makes Hazing Punishable," *Hartford Courant,* 1 July 2000; Matt Curry, "Mom Arrested for Arming Kids," *Amarillo Globe-News,* 9 March 2000. http://amarillonet. com/stories/030900/usn_armedkids.shtml
5. Hank Nuwer, ed., "Incidents and/or Allegations in the News: 2000," 23 November 2000.
6. William Joseph Whalen, *Handbook of Secret Organizations* (Milwaukee: Bruce, 1966).
7. William Graebner, "Outlawing Teenage Populism: The Campaign Against Secret Societies in the American High School, 1900-1960," *Journal of American History* 74, no. 2 (1987): 412.
8. *Ohman v. Board of Education of the City of New York*, 90 N.E.2d 474, 476 (N.Y. 1949).
9. Tracey Idell Hamilton, "When Does Hazing Cross the Line?" *Santa Maria Sun*, 19 May 2000. http://www.santamariasun.com/ archives/covers_2000/cov_05192000.html
10. Jan Padlow, "Hazing Hangs Tough, Despite Efforts to Eradicate It," *Tallahassee Democrat*, 23 February 1999.
11. Kevin Murphy, "District Settles Suit over Disciplining Football Players," *Milwaukee Journal Sentinel,* 18 May 2000, p. 2B.
12. Raymond Schroth, "Brotherhoods of Death," *America* 177 (18 October 1997): 7.
13. Lionel Tiger, *Men in Groups*, 2nd ed. (New York: M. Moyars, Scribner, 1984), p. 135.
14. Abraham H. Maslow, *Motivation and Personality* (New York: Harper & Row, 1970).
15. Anne Flowers and Edward C. Bolmeier, *Law and Pupil Control* (Cincinnati: W.H. Anderson, 1964), pp. 12-13.

16. Michael L. Levin, "Hazing: Debunking the Myths About This 'Right' of Passage," *Updating School Policies* 31, no. 2 (May 2000).
17. *Mayo Clinic Health Letter,* September 1989, p. 7.
18. Bryan A. Garner, ed., *Black's Law Dictionary*, 7th ed. (St. Paul, Minn.: West, 1999), p. 100.
19. Ibid., p. 1497.
20. Ibid., p. 1056.
21. *Featherston* v. *Allstate Insurance,* 875 P.2d 937, 940 (Idaho 1994).
22. *Rupp* v. *Bryant,* 417 So. 2d 658 (Fla.1982), 668.
23. *Bryant* v. *School Board of Duval County,* 399 So. 2d 417, 417 (Fla. 1981).
24. *McNaughton* v. *Circleville Board of Education*, 345 N.E.2d 649, 656 (Ohio 1974).
25. Garner, op. cit., p. 753.
26. *Ledfors* v. *Emery County School District,* 849 P.2d 1162, 1167 (Utah 1993).
27. Scott R. Rosner and R. Brian Crow, "Institutional Liability for Hazing in Interscholastic Sports," *Houston Law Review* 39 (2002): 296.
28. Associated Press, "Six Coaches Resign in Wake of Hazing Investigation," 27 May 2000; Mark Shaffer, "Winslow Coach Indicted in Hazing," *Arizona Republic,* 23 May 2000, p. A1.
29. Associated Press, "Six Starters Out for Eagles in Friday Football Game," 28 September 2000. "Police News," *Hartford Courant,* 26 September 2000.
30. Associated Press, "Investigation into High School Hazings Nets Arrest," 25 May 2000; Staff, "Students Face Hazing Charges," *State Journal Register*, 24 May 2000, p. 13.
31. *Rupp,* p. 661.
32. Ibid., p. 669.
33. Eric Vaughn and Matt Curry, "Authorities Investigate Alleged Hazing," *Amarillo Globe-News*, 18 September 1996. http://amarillonet.com/news/perryton91896.html; Chip Chandler, "Teen Acquitted in Hazing Case," *Amarillo Globe-News*, 29 May 1997. http://amarillonet.com/stories/052997/teen.html
34. UPI, "Principal Faces Suspension over Hazing," 30 January 1988.
35. UPI, "Coaches Ousted Over Hazing Rite," *New York Times*, 3

December 1981, p. B24; ESPN.com and Hank Nuwer, "Sports Hazing Incidents," *ESPN.com*, 3 June 2000. http://espn.go.com/otl/hazing/list.html

36. Rob Hotakainen and Gregor W. Pinney, "Mom, Teen Push for Anti-hazing Bill," *Star Tribune,* 17 January 1997, p. 1B; Kermit Pattison, "Minnesota Grapples with How to Curb Hazing in High School," *Christian Science Monitor,* 4 February 1997, p. 3.

37. Gene Fadness, "Students Shouldn't Have to Endure Humiliation at School," *Idaho Falls Post Register*, 21 December 1994, p. A7; Jim Fisher, "In Shoshone, the High School Licenses Its Bullies," *Lewiston Morning Tribune,* 20 December 1994, p. 10A.

38. Juan Williams, "Analysis: Persistence of Hazing and the Increase of Incidents Involving Teens," *Talk of the Nation*, 28 March 2000.

39. Art Taylor, Sport in Society. www.sportinsociety.org

40. *McNaughton*, p. 657.

APPENDIX A

Hazing Statutes

At the time of publication, 43 states have laws on the books specifically addressing hazing. The following tables present information gleaned from each state's hazing laws. During the distillation process, which was necessary in order to place information in a table format, many nuances and details of a particular state's hazing statute had to be excluded. Readers should consult the specific statute for more detailed information.

Table 1. Statute and class of offense.

State	Statute	Year Enacted	Remedy/Class of Offense
Alabama	§ 16-1-23	1998	Class C
Alaska	No statute	No statute	No statute
Arizona	§ 15-2301	2001	Not stated
Arkansas	§ 6-5-201	1983	Class B
California	§ 32050	1976	Yes
Colorado	§ 18-9-124	1999	Class 3 misdemeanor
Connecticut	§ 53-23a	1999	Not stated
Delaware	§ 9301	1992	Class B
Florida	§ 240.1325	1990	Not stated
Georgia	§ 16-5-61	1988	High /aggravated misdemeanor
Hawaii	No statute	No statute	No statute
Idaho	§ 18-917	1991	Misdemeanor
Illinois	§ 720 ILCS 120	1901	Class A misdemeanor or Class 4 felony (death)
Indiana	§ 34-30-2-150	1998	Class B misdemeanor — Class C felony (deadly weapon)
Iowa	§ 708.10	1999	Simple misdemeanor — serious misdemeanor
Kansas	§ 21-3434	1986	Class B non-person misdemeanor

Kentucky	§ 164.375	1986	Not stated
Louisiana	§ 1801	1920	Not stated
Maine	§ 6553	1999	Civil/Criminal
Maryland	§ 268H	1985	Misdemeanor
Massachusetts	§ 269:17	1985	Not stated
Michigan	No statute	No statute	No statute
Minnesota	§ 121A.69	1997	Not stated
Mississippi	§ 97-3-105	1990	1st or 2nd degree misdemeanor
Missouri	§ 578.360	1987	Class A misdemeanor—Class C felony (harm)
Montana	No statute	No statute	No statute
Nebraska	§ 28-311.06	1994	Class II misdemeanor
Nevada	§ 200.605	1999	Misdemeanor — gross misdemeanor
New Hampshire	§ 631:7	1993	Class B misdemeanor
New Jersey	§ 2C: 40-3	1991	4th degree misdemeanor
New Mexico	No statute	No statute	No statute
New York	§ 120:16	1988	1st or 2nd degree misdemeanor
North Carolina	§ 14.35	1913	Misdemeanor
North Dakota	§ 12.1-17.10	1995	Class B misdemeanor
Ohio	§ 2903.31	1983	Not stated
Oklahoma	§ 1190	1990	Misdemeanor
Oregon	§ 163.197	1983	Individual, Class B misdemeanor - Organization, Class A misdemeanor
Pennsylvania	§ 5352	1986	3rd degree misdemeanor
Rhode Island	§ 11-21-1	1909	Misdemeanor
South Carolina	§ 16-3-5-10	1987	Not stated
South Dakota	No statute	No statute	No statute
Tennessee	§ 49-7-123	1995	Not stated
Texas	§ 37.152	1995	Misdemeanor
Utah	§ 76-5-107.5	1953	Class C misdemeanor — 2nd degree felony (dangerous weapon)
Vermont	§ 140b	1999	Not stated
Virginia	§ 18.2-56	1950	Class 1 misdemeanor
Washington	§ 28B.10.900	1993	Misdemeanor
West Virginia	§ 18-16-3	1995	Not stated
Wisconsin	§ 948-51	1983	Class A misdemeanor — Class E felony (harm)
Wyoming	No statute	No statute	No statute

Table 2. Statutory analysis, part 1.

State	Addresses On- or Off- Campus Hazing	Statute Covers	Failure to Report Penalty Applicable	Hazers Shall Be Expelled
Alabama	Yes	High School/College	Yes	No
Alaska	No statute	No statute	No statute	No statute
Arizona	N/A	High School/College	No	No
Arkansas	Yes	High School/College	Yes	Yes
California	No	High School/College	No	No
Colorado	N/A	N/A	N/A	N/A
Connecticut	N/A	College only	N/A	Yes (one year)
Delaware	Yes	College only	N/A	N/A
Florida	Yes	College only	N/A	N/A
Georgia	N/A	High School/College	N/A	N/A
Hawaii	No statute	No statute	No statute	No statute
Idaho	N/A	College only	N/A	N/A
Illinois	N/A	High School/College	N/A	N/A
Indiana	N/A	General	Yes	N/A
Iowa	N/A	High School/College	N/A	N/A
Kansas	N/A	Social/Fraternal	N/A	N/A
Kentucky	N/A	College only	N/A	N/A
Louisiana	N/A	High School/College	No	Yes
Maine	N/A	High School/College	N/A	N/A
Maryland	N/A	High School/College	N/A	N/A
Massachusetts	N/A	High School/College	Yes	N/A
Michigan	No statute	No statute	No statute	No statute
Minnesota	Yes	High School/College	N/A	N/A
Mississippi	Yes	High School/College	N/A	N/A
Missouri	Yes	College only	N/A	N/A
Montana	No statute	No statute	No statute	No statute
Nebraska	N/A	College only	N/A	N/A
Nevada	N/A	High School/College	N/A	N/A
New Hampshire	N/A	High School/College	Yes	N/A
New Jersey	N/A	College/Fraternal	N/A	N/A
New Mexico	No statute	No statute	No statute	No statute
New York	N/A	N/A	N/A	N/A
North Carolina	N/A	College only	N/A	Yes
North Dakota	N/A	N/A	N/A	N/A
Ohio	N/A	High School/College	N/A	N/A

Oklahoma	N/A	High School/College	N/A	N/A
Oregon	N/A	College only	N/A	N/A
Pennsylvania	Yes	College only	N/A	N/A
Rhode Island	Yes	N/A	N/A	N/A
South Carolina	N/A	College only	N/A	May be expelled
South Dakota	No statute	No statute	No statute	No statute
Tennessee	Yes	College only	N/A	N/A
Texas	Yes	High School/College	Yes	N/A
Utah	N/A	N/A	N/A	N/A
Vermont	N/A	High School/College	N/A	N/A
Virginia	N/A	High School/College	Yes	Yes
Washington	N/A	College only	N/A	N/A
West Virginia	N/A	N/A	N/A	N/A
Wisconsin	N/A	N/A	N/A	N/A
Wyoming	No statute	No statute	No statute	No statute

Table 3. Statutory analysis, part 2.

State	Fine	Comprehensive Definition?[1]	Bodily Harm Addressed	Consent as a Defense?
Alabama	N/A	Yes	N/A	N/A
Alaska	No statute	No statute	No statute	No statute
Arizona	N/A	Yes	No	No
Arkansas	N/A	No	N/A	N/A
California	$100 - $5,000	No	Yes	N/A
Colorado	N/A	Yes	Yes	No
Connecticut	$1,000 - $1,500	Yes	Yes	No
Delaware	N/A	Yes	N/A	N/A
Florida	N/A	Yes	N/A	N/A
Georgia	N/A	No	N/A	N/A
Hawaii	No statute	No statute	No statute	No statute
Idaho	N/A	Yes	Yes	N/A
Illinois	N/A	No	Yes	N/A
Indiana	N/A	No	Yes	N/A
Iowa	N/A	No	Yes	No
Kansas	N/A	No	Yes	No
Kentucky	N/A	Yes	No	N/A
Louisiana	$10 - $100	No	No	No
Maine	N/A	Yes	N/A	N/A

Maryland	$500	No	No	No
Massachusetts	Up to $3,000	Yes	Yes	No
Michigan	No statute	No statute	No statute	No statute
Minnesota	N/A	No	No	No
Mississippi	$2,000	No	Yes	N/A
Missouri	N/A	No	Yes	No
Montana	No statute	No statute	No statute	No statute
Nebraska	Up to $10,000	No	N/A	No
Nevada	N/A	No	N/A	No
New Hampshire	N/A	No	N/A	No
New Jersey	N/A	No	N/A	No
New Mexico	No statute	No statute	No statute	No statute
New York	N/A	No	N/A	N/A
North Carolina	$500	No	N/A	N/A
North Dakota	N/A	No	N/A	N/A
Ohio	N/A	No	N/A	N/A
Oklahoma	$1,500	Yes	N/A	N/A
Oregon	$250 - $1,000	No	N/A	N/A
Pennsylvania	N/A	No	N/A	N/A
Rhode Island	$500	No	N/A	N/A
South Carolina	N/A	No	N/A	N/A
South Dakota	No statute	No statute	No statute	No statute
Tennessee	N/A	No	N/A	N/A
Texas	$1,000 - $10,000	Yes	N/A	No
Utah	N/A	Yes	Yes	N/A
Vermont	N/A	Yes	N/A	No
Virginia	N/A	No	N/A	N/A
Washington	N/A	No	N/A	N/A
West Virginia	N/A	No	N/A	N/A
Wisconsin	N/A	No	N/A	N/A
Wyoming	No statute	No statute	No statute	No statute

[1]The more specific the statute, the greater chance a "Yes" is indicated in this column.

Table 4. Statutory analysis, part 3.

State	Must Have Written Policy	Other State-Specific Information
Alabama	N/A	Forfeit scholarship if applicable
Alaska	No statute	No statute

Arizona	Yes	Solicitation to engage in hazing is prohibited
Arkansas	N/A	
California	N/A	Addresses "pre-initiation"
Colorado	N/A	Passed to cover gap in criminal statutes
Connecticut	N/A	Individual fined, organization fined
Delaware	N/A	Withhold transcripts until fines are paid
Florida	Yes	Withhold transcripts until fines are paid
Georgia	N/A	
Hawaii	No statute	No statute
Idaho	N/A	
Illinois	N/A	Unless acts are sanctioned
Indiana	N/A	
Iowa	N/A	
Kansas	N/A	
Kentucky	Yes	Policy must cover visitors on campus
Louisiana	N/A	
Maine	Yes	Rules must be in by-laws of organization
Maryland	N/A	Up to one year imprisonment
Massachusetts	Yes	Yearly notification of statute to students
Michigan	No statute	No statute
Minnesota	Yes	Includes staff hazing
Mississippi	Yes	
Missouri	N/A	
Montana	No statute	No statute
Nebraska	N/A	
Nevada	N/A	
New Hampshire	N/A	Phrases, "knowingly participates" and "if hazed and fail to report"
New Jersey	N/A	Developed "Pledge Bill of Rights"
New Mexico	No statute	No statute
New York	N/A	
North Carolina	N/A	If fail to expel, administrator is guilty of misdemeanor
North Dakota	N/A	
Ohio	N/A	If employees found liable, institution may be held liable
Oklahoma	N/A	
Oregon	N/A	Separate fines for individual and organization
Pennsylvania	Yes	Withhold transcripts until fines are paid

Rhode Island	N/A	Administrator guilty of misdemeanor if knowingly allows hazing
South Carolina	N/A	
South Dakota	No statute	No statute
Tennessee	Yes	Policy must be distributed annually
Texas	Yes	$1,000 fine for failing to report hazing
Utah	N/A	Failing to report by licensed person is "unprofessional practice"
Vermont	N/A	
Virginia	N/A	Civil and criminal offense
Washington	Yes	Forfeit scholarship if guilty of hazing
West Virginia	N/A	
Wisconsin	N/A	
Wyoming	No statute	No statute

Chronology of Cases Related to Secret Societies

Steele v. *Sexton*, 234 N.W. 426 (Mich. 1931)

In *Steele* v. *Sexton*, the critical question was whether a school had the authority to withhold academic credit from students who belong to a secret society, thereby preventing them from graduating. Steele, a senior, contended that this consequence was cruel and unusual punishment and in violation of the Eighth Amendment to the U.S. Constitution. Steele admitted to the principal and superintendent that he was a member of Phi Epsilon. Michigan laws in 1931 forbade membership in this type of high school fraternity. Punishment for those who defied the law included suspension, expulsion, or withholding credit. School officials permitted Steele to continue to attend classes, but they withheld credit for the classes. Steele was not permitted to graduate because he did not have enough credits to fulfill the graduation requirements. In order to answer the question before it, the court needed to determine whether the credits represented a property interest and, if so, whether the school unconstitutionally denied Steele this property interest. In finding for the school district, the majority held: "The right to attend the educational institutions of the state is not a natural right. It is a gift of civilization, a benefaction of the law. If a person seeks to become a beneficiary of this gift, he must submit to such conditions as the law imposes as a condition precedent to this right" (*Id.* at 830). Although not part of the holding of this case, the dissenting opinion has become important in that various courts have used it as a basis for arguing that the loss of a property right violates state and federal law:

> Credits, which a pupil has earned, are valuable. These credits are property. This law arbitrarily interferes with the sphere of individual liberty, guaranteed by the constitution, seeks to establish unjust, unreasonable and arbitrary rules of social conduct and deprives the pupil and his parents of property, in violation of the Constitution of this state and of the Fourteenth Amendment of the Constitution of the United States (*Id.* at 440).

Antell v. *Stokes,* 191 N.E. 407 (Mass. 1934)

In *Antell* v. *Stokes,* a student sought reinstatement after school officials suspended her for violating a school policy banning membership in secret societies. The policy was very clear as to what the consequences would be if school officials found a pupil to be a member of a secret society. The court, in finding that the board of education had the right to implement the policy and to exclude the student for violating the rule, stated, "The power to make rules would be vain without the capacity to annex reasonable penalties for their violation" (*Id.* at 409). Thus Antell affirmed the legal right of boards of education to make reasonable rules governing students' actions when those actions are found to be disruptive to the educational process.

Coggins v. *Board,* 28 S.E.2d 527 (N.C. 1944)

In *Coggins* v. *Board,* the court was asked to determine whether a board of education has the right to bar students that belong to a Greek letter society from participating in extracurricular activities. The court found that a board of education does have the right to establish such a rule. The court further found that by exercising this right, the board would not be denying students an education. The court, basically, placed the decision on the individual student. The student could belong to a Greek letter society, but that would prohibit him from participating in school-sponsored organizations. On the other hand, if the student wanted to participate in school-sponsored activities, one of the stipulations would be that he would not be able to belong to a Greek letter society.

Satan v. *Board of Public Instruction*, 22 So. 2d 892 (Fla. 1945)

A Florida court, in *Satan* v. *Board of Public Instruction*, supported the position that courts should not interfere with the operation of a school system unless unreasonable restrictions are in place. Under the laws of Florida, conduct and disciplinary issues are the responsibility of the county boards of public instruction. The courts have indicated that as long as disciplinary measures imposed by county boards are reasonable, they will not be disturbed.

Burkitt v. *School District No. 1, Multnomah County*, 246 P.2d 566 (Ore. 1952)

The legal questions illustrated in this case deal with the degree of secrecy necessary for a group to be considered a secret society. The court reaffirmed the right of a board of education to forbid membership in a secret society and to exclude students that choose to become members. However, the predominant question in this case was just how secret an organization had to be in order for it to be classified as a secret society. The court determined that any of the following elements would be enough to classify the organization a secret society: "a pledge or an oath not to reveal the secrets of the society, a secret password or grip, rituals, including initiation ceremonies, which members are under an obligation not to disclose" (*Id.* at 572). *Burkitt* also affirmed a superintendent's right to regulate student organizations whether they are determined to be secret societies or not. As long as the superintendent believes the student organization is acting in a manner "inimical to the best interests of the school pupils, the community, or the effective operation of the schools" (*Id.* at 579), the superintendent has the power to restrict the activities of that organization.

Holroyd v. *Eibling*, 188 N.E.2d 797 (Ohio Ct. App. 1962)

In *Holroyd* v. *Eibling*, high school students and their parents challenged the board of education's enforcement of a regulation that prohibits students from affiliating with social clubs. Students found violating this regulation were to be barred from participating in extracurricular activities. The students claimed that by allowing this regulation to stand, the board would be in complete control of the students' activities throughout the entire year, including summer recess. However, the court upheld the board's authority to enforce the regulation pursuant to section 3313.20 of the Ohio Revised Code. That statute provides: "the board of education shall make such rules, and regulations as are necessary for its government and the government of its employees and the pupils of the school" (*Id*. at 800).

ABOUT THE AUTHORS

Kevin L. Guynn is director of the Office for Exceptional Children in the Chardon Local School District in Ohio. Guynn has 25 years of experience as an educator in the Ohio public schools. Fourteen of those years were as a high school band director. His Ph.D. in urban education is from Cleveland State University.

Frank D. Aquila is a professor of educational administration at Cleveland State University and a practicing lawyer. Aquila teaches courses in law, collective bargaining, and school facilities and staff development. His latest book, *Law for Educators,* will be published in January 2005. He recently received the John Glenn Scholars in Service Award for his work with service learning. Aquila has a Ph.D. in educational administration from Kent State University and a J.D. from the Cleveland-Marshall School of Law.